Authorized Visitors

Karen,
   A wonderful poet and an inspiration to me

Nancy Jentsch
May 2017

Authorized Visitors

Poems by Nancy K. Jentsch

Cherry Grove Collections

© 2017 by Nancy K. Jentsch

Published by Cherry Grove Collections
P.O. Box 541106
Cincinnati, OH 45254-1106

ISBN: 9781625492333

Poetry Editor: Kevin Walzer
Business Editor: Lori Jareo

Visit us on the web at www.cherry-grove.com

Acknowledgments

I am grateful to the following journals where these poems first appeared, some in slightly different versions.

the Aurorean: "Brambleberry" and "Harbingers"
For a Better World: Poems and Drawings on Peace and Justice: "Managua por la mañana" and "Snapshot"
Panoply: "What to Pack for the Autumnal Equinox"
Postcard Poems and Prose: "Pine Cones on My Window Sill"
Route 7 Review: "Untamed Sweetness"
Star 82 Review: "All Brains and Thumbs" and "Authorized Visitors"

I would like to thank my fellow poets, Donelle Dreese, Karen George and Taunja Thomson for their support and invaluable help in the crafting of many of the poems in this collection.

I would also like to thank my husband Philip and my sister Lynda for reading my manuscript, making suggestions and supporting me every step of the way.

In memory of my mother, who pulled "*A Child's Garden of Verses* from her past," and sowed my childhood with its seeds.

Table of Contents

Untamed Sweetness..11
Harbingers..12
All Brains and Thumbs...13
Late Afternoon Cypress..14
Her Flight or Mine?..15
On a Country Road in Spring...................................16
Happenstance..17
Down the Middle...18
Authorized Visitors..19
What Makes the Book Better Than the Movie.........20
Hands of Altamira..21
Twice a River...22
Waterways..23
Evolution..24
Brambleberry...25
Layer Cake Sunset...26
Windowless Sight..27
Pine Cones on My Window Sill...............................28
Phoebe's Blessing..29
Sparrows' Passage...30
Managua por la mañana..31
Snapshot..32
For Gisèle..33
White Lichens...34
What Matters..35
Unexpected Elegies..36
What to Pack for the Autumnal Equinox................37
Past Twilight..38
At Pond's Edge...39
Of Towhee and Ginger...40
Last May's Poem..41

Untamed Sweetness

Black raspberries ripen wild at creek's edge
my eyes close, lips tingle
to memories of brimming backyard bushes.

These untended berry-gems hide tiny
behind stickers   beyond reach.
I bend the canes to mine the ready flesh

lest deer or songbirds steal
the pear-fed coyote plunder.
At day's end, red-lipped,

I leave a fruit or two of untamed sweetness
like words that stray from verses
and still are pearls.

Harbingers

The first spring birdsong
cuts diamond sharp
through morning's misty start
reflects Onkel Martin's
memory: how the first whistled
tune since war's end
rose above jagged rubble
woke from smoke-gray dreams

All Brains and Thumbs

an arched branch fell
with the first winter storm,
now anchored by inch
after inch of snow—a cardinal's
perch where he awaits
a place at the feeder,
keeps clenched claws dry

if only I, with my brain-stuffed skull
and opposable thumbs could
grasp at chance as
firmly as he

Late Afternoon Cypress

Just now the sun
caught the crown
of the cypress.
Branches wear
bronze coins bold
against untroubled
bluet sky,
glint and lilt
with the breeze,
taunt my eyes
like a lost memory
mocks my mind.

Her Flight or Mine?

I stand in awe
of the shell-bound gosling
whose feathers might fly
her ungainly shape
over peak-trimmed lakes
that await her call
or stuff a comforter
with enough loft
to incubate my dreams
in a fifty-degree room
so I can trek mountains
or spin in pirouette

On a Country Road in Spring

songbird's urgent search for love
airy dance step
atop grounded pole
riff reiterates
eyes and ears rivet
on lust-filled trills

unmuffled motorcycle passes
driver's purpose no different

Happenstance

A stone skims the lake's bronze
lands lighthearted
in a frame of umber rushes

Roadside weeds, christened in spring
dare to bloom
as a palette peppered with mischief

Happenstance unfolds moments
soaked with nectar
prized like November's daisy
while calendar squares march
and second hands turn
unable to decant grandeur

Down the Middle

When the dental hygienist
asks how I am
I take her along

a flat asphalt track
of smooth gray facts.
Down the middle

two slick yellow lines
draw my words taut.
They stray neither

to the road's broken edge,
a jagged magnet for trash,
nor to the unruly

jewels just beyond, that root
bloom and twist with the sun
in just one season.

No mention is made
of evening's misty amethyst
a melody of wishes

tomorrow's dawn
might well dissolve.

Authorized Visitors

Hoof prints by the sign
"Authorized Visitors Only"
told me there had been other
trespassers here.
Would the doe have been prosecuted
the doe who wanted a cool sip
of river water before climbing
the bank to birth a fawn?
Are birds overhead
required to change their love song
to a call of warning
on their visaless flight?
Could the sun's lawyers plead for leniency
though their client shines above the law
joins sand and wind to erase
all signs of words?
What about the water
transgressing the sand
at the sign's edge
ridging a mat
of unparalleled undulations
to welcome visitors
authorized or not?

What Makes the Book Better Than the Movie

I could have a chicken cam in the coop
        to see who wakes the flock with the first clucks of dawn
        to watch who nudges whom out of the nest box
        to find out how a hen fights her way
                to the highest point of the roost
                      for the night.

But it's enough to hear the sounds of waking and imagine
        the fluffing of feather frocks
        the early morning chat
        the strut from roost to nest box
        the dreamy gaze as the egg is laid
        the afternoon tea party
                with all the girls sharing tales
                of what they think I am up to.

Hands of Altamira

Cardinal's nest plucked from honeysuckle
placed proudly on bedroom shelf
or waterfall brushed on canvas
framed and hung at show

      Nature snatched from its context
      tamed, dried, bottled, transcribed
      the ageless zeal that fueled
      the hands of Altamira

Violins trill like a lovesick wood thrush
      master of his home-school aria
Perfume smiles with the lightness of lilacs
      as evening lids the day
Tulips, pieced and quilted, blanket winter with spring
      their loft a welcome house guest
Pixels capture mountain shadows on matte paper
      lend us calm for office walls
Even verses walk a garden path
      feast on nectar, nest in catnip's shadow

Twice a River

A river sketch
holds water's breath

stills the millrace
with pen-stroke fetters

which eyes and mind
unleash in spills and splashes

while a poem of ink on paper
floats on waves of wind

wears trilling birds
settles them on branches

where leaves, river-reflected
in restive umber

beckon twice

Waterways

1962
A water snake's fangs
shock an ankle deep in innocence.
Imagined venom
etches fear,
my childhood veers to higher ground
away from creek water dangers.

1985
In divided Germany
barges course veins
that ignore borders.
I walk east hailed
by exotic flags till halted
by mines, *Todesstreifen*, razor wire.

1889
The Rhine boarded
Omama's family
on course for Reading's factories
where the Schuylkill paid wages
made promises of perpetuity
but remains her sole *in situ* survivor.

1987
Like the Ohio I find my way
from one commonwealth to another
till I settle along a creek
where arrowheads wash up
rubber boots guard innocent feet
dare snapping turtles.

Evolution

Urchin-covered rocks turned red with age
rely on the tender rinse of undercurrents

Spiny dancers flirt and balance, Virginia Reel partners
nurtured by velvet waves keeping time

Moon-fed tides court bladed fins in a rhythmic
ritual under the cover of rocky shadows

My smooth cheeks, your chin's stubble
each would wilt without the other

Brambleberry

Late afternoon brambleberry
leads me to a creek bed
        that winds
        loops back
        wanders from me
on its way through the watershed.
Otter-brown leaves stray
in the maze of timber whose aged bark
is a puzzle with no solution.

Twilight follows dusk
I twirl in place
exulting in lostness
willing no gridlines.
White moonlight in inky sky
welcomes my dance.

Layer Cake Sunset

Layer cake sunset
      iced by cedar-berry blue
last wisps of buttery warmth
        from squinting sun
           before winter's fires kindle wishes
              lights frame evening, then night
              down comforts slumber
              dreams float like chilled breath
                  sketch confections on cold black panes
                  sweeten sleepy sunrise

Windowless Sight

How did assembly-line designers
in a windowless scarf factory
know that pink and gray
play a divine duet,
echo an aria of clouds
(floating on a cherry ostinato)
that blushed, then hid
on the heels of a clever
breeze, rushed
toward night's cadence

Pine Cones on My Window Sill

some unfold early with bold curves that spill inner treasures
others fill space locked tight cold on the sill

then a surprise rich as lavender blackberry jam—
the closed cones stretch and pop

expel jewels from within
my sill made warm with sound and seed

Phoebe's Blessing

At dawn the phoebe
wobbles on a wire
rasps *Amen, Amen*
to my restive night
heaps my hungry hands
with a bouquet of birdsong
I scatter
across my day

Sparrows' Passage

Stowaway sparrows
drawn by sails' wake
made landfall in the Colonies
settled impatient vastness
alongside farmers city builders traders
Today these Old World passeridae
invasive as purple loosestrife
snap at scraps in airports
held by glass and steel
while I mount clouds
ride air currents
with patterns
that recall
rigging

Managua por la mañana

Morning sounds in Managua
move my sleep towards light.
My dreams dawn to thoughts
as rooster's kikirikí inspires
tropical birds to trills as fanciful as their plumage.
Trucks labor uphill spewing
fumes and off-key fugues in their wake.
From behind the compound's scissor-wire-trimmed wall
our protector barks.
I should feel safe.
Managua por la mañana.

Against this backdrop enter voices
voices chanting slogans
voices marching in unison
under a choking cloud of smoking rubber.
My liminal senses perceive
reprise of revolution in Nicaragua
and fear sears my weary synapses.

Gathering courage I wake
and hear beyond the mirage
doves cooing in unison,
roosting above the embers that warmed the poor of
Managua
into tomorrow.
Mañana en Managua.

Snapshot

My lens catches an oxcart
(fortuitously framed by a thatched roof,
in the background a white beach,
cresting waves of the Pacific)
burdened with driftwood—
smoky heat for the chill of the night
(a sure first prize in the international category).

The prize pocketed,
a thought as scorching as the sun over Nicaragua
causes me to hide the picture,
ashamed I'd found the scene quaint
when its actors' roles were daunting,
heaving wood on the treadmill of survival
with fuel for a night's fire the sole reward.
I'd prized only the tableau,
pixels framed by thatch
before the drumbeat of the ocean's waves.

For Gisèle

The morning glistened

I pressed a lavender stalk for you in a book
sipped from a pot of jasmine pearls on my porch
against a backdrop of chatting birds
and hens attending the lawn

I welcomed morning's warmth while hanging wash
but the day changed by the proverbial threes
a mower's motor crashed into gear
the laundry line collapsed
the last five socks didn't match

I parried by threes and knelt among yarrow's cleansing scent
then sweated my way to the shady creek bank
seeking the last wild berries,
and there recalled the bit of my glistening morning,
facing the pages,
awaiting your touch

White Lichens

My eyes graze on flowers of white—
the last daisies, a latch-hook carpet of clover,
the summer's first Queen Anne's lace.
Frail dancers the wind invites to a quick pirouette,

they beckon me to the wall he stacked
rock upon rock with passion and perspicacity,
a labor he willed never to finish,
so paired were the pulses of man and rock.
But man's pulses ceased and a year ago at the cusp of the seasons
his ashes were here sown,

white lichens, reunited with these wrinkled Ordovician remains,
eager for a dance with the wind.

What Matters

If you'd deadheaded the marigolds
more often this summer
would they have bloomed a day longer

spread into a fanciful checkerboard
for twenty-four more hours?

And if it had rained that last day
before the fall's first killing frost
weighing the puffy blooms into nods

not even Van Gogh could salvage
what would have been won?

Your breaths are numbered like the days
between first and last frosts
the extra day of bloom matters

only if the sight of it
quickened your pulse.

Unexpected Elegies

When weeds crowd my lavender mounds
I laugh
and pull them, swooning as sweetness
scatters from blooms heavy with hue

When worms hide in the cherries
I smile
and will time to stop, skimming through many
for the few that sparkle tart and pure

When a dry spell drags its feet
I skip
and aim the hose, one with water pulsing
to still the begging petals and stems

When tarnished skies tip their ballast
I grin
and sip milky tea, etch a waiting page
with unexpected elegies

What to Pack for the Autumnal Equinox

     stopped clock
for time to listen for falling leaves
staccato sparks of burning twigs

     roomy shoes
for a walk in search
of September's solitary daisy

     clothes line and pins
to drip dry what the year has soaked
in loss and flaunted dreams

     bushel basket
light with warmth of the day
the green beans got canned

     kaleidoscope
weighted with late-summer seeds
cascading portents of spring

     fleece blocks
quilted with wise stitches
to welcome the coming cold

     breath of lavender
to spice our pillow for the night
when dark and light make peace

Past Twilight

Sun's last breath into clouds from below
etches their uneasy outlines white hot
Stark shapes beyond Kandinsky's ken
startle the horizon till colors

that escaped a rainbow
warm lake's satin nightgown
with hints of taffeta
smooth as the memories
we choose to swaddle us
past twilight

At Pond's Edge

We fished at my dawn
Your picture of a towhead

silent in red corduroy overalls
feeds our memory

Morning light warms
the pond's rushes in the frame

hung above a lifetime
tossed by rapids into channeled flow

till you stand by the rushes
rinsed of words

contemplate the plunge
into heaven's womb

Of Towhee and Ginger

My mother pulls
A Child's Garden of Verses
from her past, and embraced
by Stevenson's cadences
I swing my legs in rhythm
imagine colors cascading
on black and white pages
sail entranced with My Shadow
to Foreign Lands till we dock
At the Seaside or the Land of Nod

Now as a young Towhee
discovers her trill
I unlid words
hidden for half a century
like homely spring blooms
of Wild Ginger
under life's leaf mold:

> Wild Ginger rings its hidden chimes
> bids Wood Peewee and Towhee
> to chat upon the Buckeye
>
> Beneath the Shag Bark Hickory's branch
> Spring Beauty yields to June's shy stand
> of comely Blue-eyed Grass
>
> Then lullabied by night's Barred Owl
> who winks at sedge and cress
> the Poplar's tulips fall

Last May's Poem

Words duly processed
stand rigid on disc
while sycamores budded
leafed and leaves fell
velvet over flood-cleaned
soil, saplings pleaded
with sun and underbrush
scurried in trains' wakes

Made in the USA
Columbia, SC
14 May 2017